Bible Figures

Published by ReadingforFun.net
San Antonio, Texas 78251

TABLE OF CONTENTS

Page

In the Beginning

God created heaven and earth and separated light from darkness. The world was with water and land. The land had vegetation and living animals and the water was with an abundance of sea creatures.

God made man and woman in his likeness to have dominion over all on earth and water.

Noah Builds an Ark

Mankind became corrupt and God told Noah to build an ark for He would destroy every living creature on earth by a flood. Noah took his family, food, and two of each animal.

The Tower of Babel

Following the Great Flood, humanity spoke one single language and migrated eastward. There, they started to build a tall tower that would reach the heavens. When God saw their arrogance, he created different languages so they could no longer understand each other. They then scattered around the world.

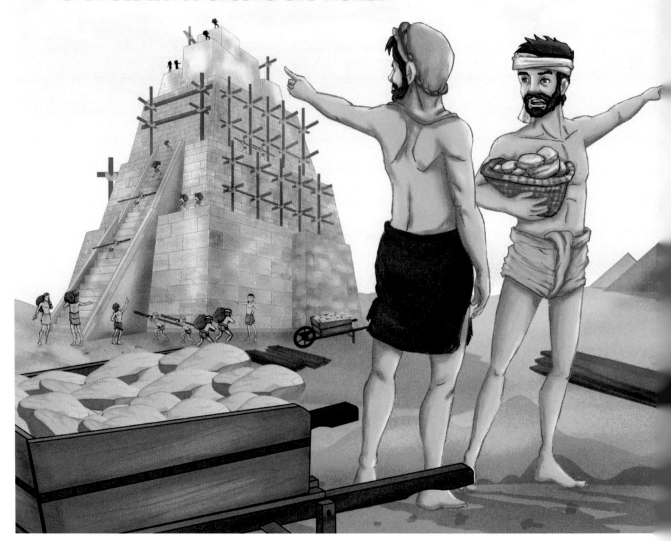

A Promise to Abraham

God chose Abraham to leave his country and kinfolk and migrate into Canaan. The Lord promised that Abraham would be the father of a great people. In Abraham, all nations should be blessed.

Joseph & the Dream

Joseph was the favorite of his father because he was the youngest child. Two dreams that Joseph had revealed that his brothers, his mother, and his father were to look up to him.

Joseph in Egypt

Joseph was one of twelve brothers favored by his father. His father made him a coat of many colors which angered his brothers. In reprisal, his brothers imprisoned him and sold him to merchants going to Egypt. Joseph became governor of Egypt because he could interpret the king's dreams.

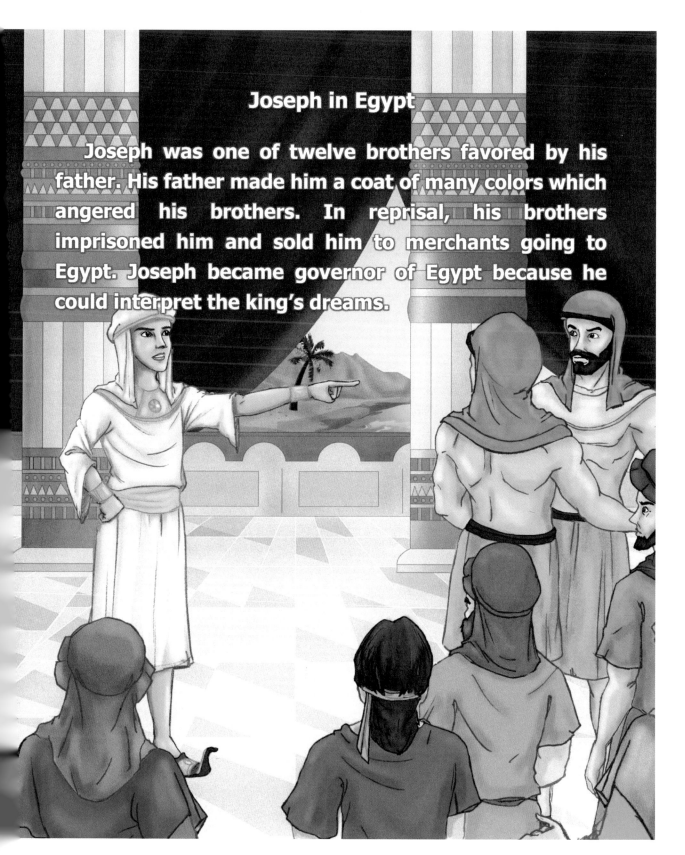

Moses

Born of a Hebrew woman, Moses was found by the Pharaoh's daughter in a floating basket on the Nile River. He was adopted and named Moses, which means "saved from the waters."

In his forties, Moses began to share the miseries of the Israelites and this angered the king. The king then commanded him to leave Egypt. God appeared to Moses in the midst of a burning bush and told him that he would lead His people out of Egypt.

Out of Egypt

Moses held out his staff, and the Red Sea was parted by God. The Israelites walked on the exposed dry ground and crossed the sea, followed by the Egyptian army. Once the Israelites crossed, Moses again moved his staff, and the sea closed again, drowning the entire Egyptian army.

The Ten Commandments

The Ten Commandments, known as the Decalogue, are a set of laws God gave the Israelites after they left Egypt.

Moses went up to Mount Sinai and came down with two tablets of stone on which the Ten Commandments were written.

Jericho

The Israelites held the walled city of Jericho under siege. The Lord commanded Joshua to have soldiers, seven priests, and the Ark led by horses circle the city for seven days. On the seventh day, the priests blew their horns, the people shouted, and the wall collapsed.

The Israelites conquered and destroyed the city, except for Rahab and her family.

Gideon

During this time, Israel was under the rule of Midian for seven years. The angel of the Lord appeared to Gideon and announced that he was the chosen one to save Israel and overthrow the Midianites. With 300 soldiers, Gideon defeated the Midian forces numbering thousands of soldiers.

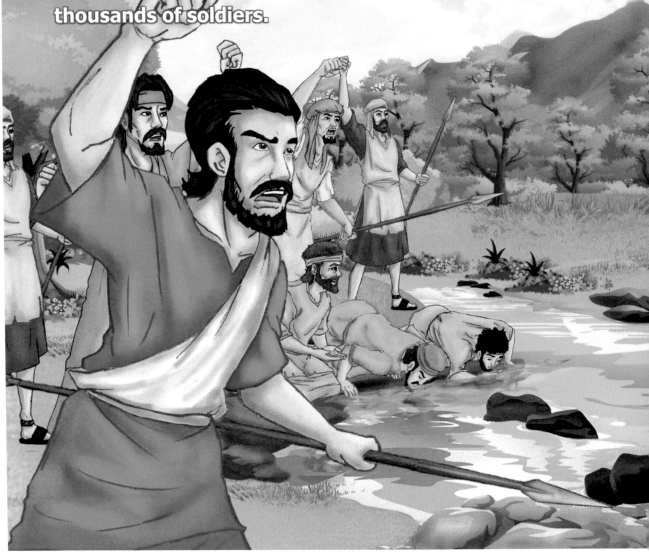

Samson

The Lord sent religious men called Judges, selected from among the people, to rule and deliver them from their enemies. One of them was Samson, a name meaning "man of the sun." He was one of the last 16 judges sent to give guidance to the ancient Israelites and was known for his super strength.

Ruth

Ruth was a Moabite woman who married into an Israelite family. After the death of her husband, she remained with his family and converted to Judaism. She said, "Where you go, I will go, and where you stay, I will stay. Your people will be my people and your God, my God."

Samuel

Samuel, whose name means "name of God," was devoted to God by his mother. As a child, he was placed in the care of Eli, high priest at the tabernacle of Shiloh.

The Lord called Samuel at a young age to become a prophet and judge of Israel and he restored law, order, and regular worship in the land.

David & Goliath

There was a battle between the Philistines and the Israelites. Goliath was champion of the Philistines and challenged anyone to battle. The King of Israel gave David permission to represent the Israelites. David's weapon was a sling and five stones.

David took a stone, hurled it, and struck Goliath on the forehead. Goliath fell lifeless on the ground. With their hero dead, the Philistines fled with the Israelites in pursuit.

David

David was chosen King of Israel. Due to his victories at war, large treasures of gold and great quantities of stolen goods were brought to Jerusalem. His kingdom extended from Egypt to the Euphrates.

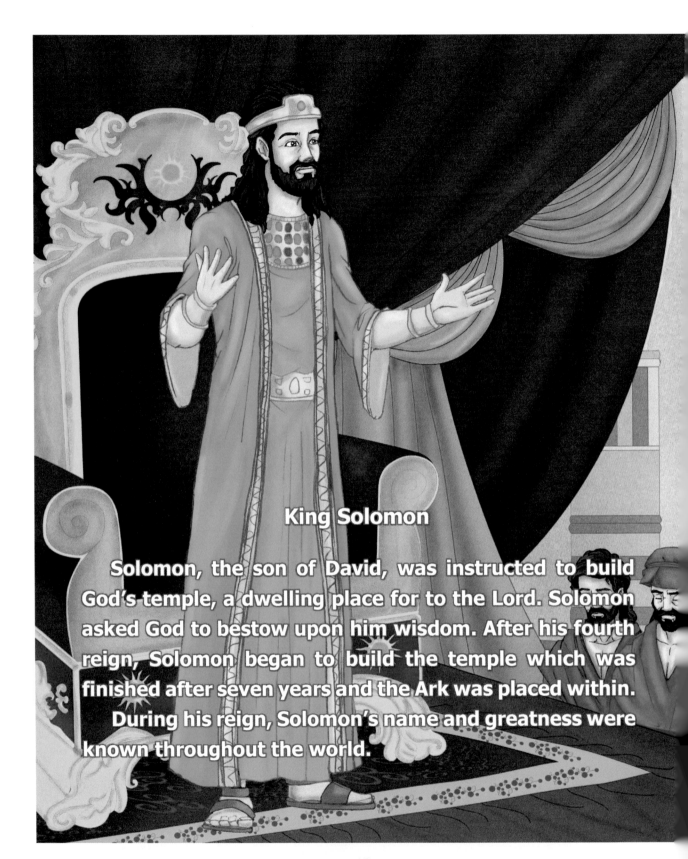

King Solomon

Solomon, the son of David, was instructed to build God's temple, a dwelling place for to the Lord. Solomon asked God to bestow upon him wisdom. After his fourth reign, Solomon began to build the temple which was finished after seven years and the Ark was placed within.

During his reign, Solomon's name and greatness were known throughout the world.

Elijah

Elijah, a prophet, spoke to Ahab, the king of Israel, and told him that a drought was to occur. The Lord then told Elijah to move to another city where a widow with a son would provide for him.

After a year of living with the widow, her son took ill. Elijah called to the Lord and life returned to the child. The widow then knew that Elijah was a man of God.

Elisha & Naaman

Elisha was a prophet of Israel in the city of Sumariah. Naaman was a leper, and the army commander of the king of Aram. He was to take silver, gold, and festal garments to the king of Israel to cure his leprosy.

Elisha sent a message for Naaman to wash seven times in the river Jordan. Naaman did as directed and his flesh was cleaned. He became a believer in the Lord of Israel.

Nehemiah

Nehemiah, a layman, rebuilt the walls of Jerusalem during the restoration period and introduced reforms. It took 52 days to accomplish this task.

Ester

Ester was a Jew who grew up as an exile in Persia. Her Jewish name was Hadassah, meaning Myrtle, which means, "Peace of Thanksgiving."

Two things she contributed to her people were to beg the king to save the Jews, which he did. This resulted in many pagans converting to Judaism.

Psalms

In the Bible, psalms are a collection of religious songs which number approximately 150. Some of these psalms were composed for the liturgy in the temple and others for recitation.

Psalms may be sung individually or in groups for the community. The most quoted psalm is Psalm 23.

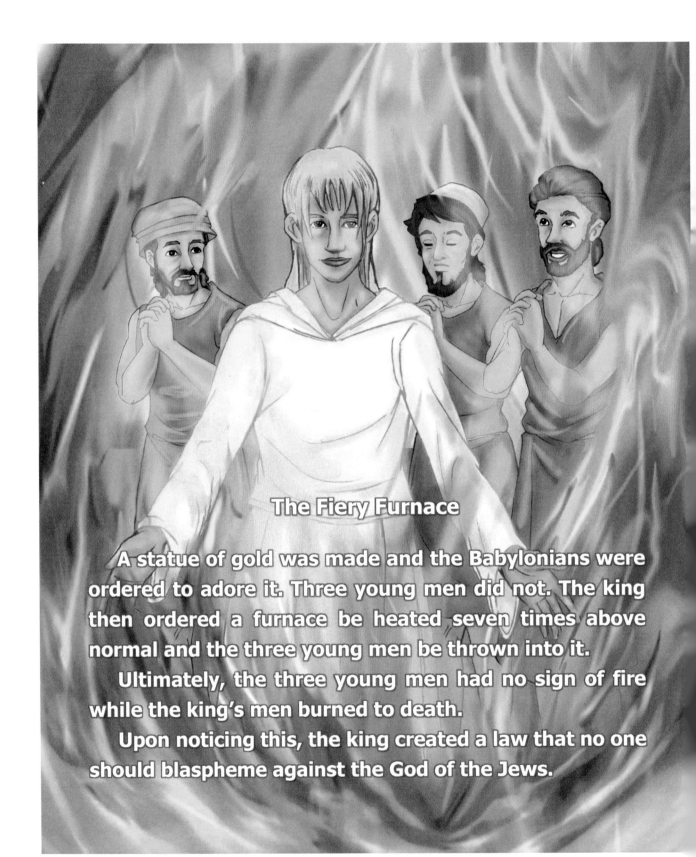

The Fiery Furnace

A statue of gold was made and the Babylonians were ordered to adore it. Three young men did not. The king then ordered a furnace be heated seven times above normal and the three young men be thrown into it.

Ultimately, the three young men had no sign of fire while the king's men burned to death.

Upon noticing this, the king created a law that no one should blaspheme against the God of the Jews.

Jonah

God commanded Jonah to go to the city of Nimve. Jonah disobeyed and fled on a boat, fell into the sea, and was swallowed by a whale. For three days and nights, Jonah was in the belly of the whale.

On the last day, Jonah was expelled from the whale. God told Jonah a second time to go to Nimve and preach penance to the people for their sins.

In the Lions' Den

After Daniel was taken captive and put him into the lion's den for seven days, the king noticed that Daniel was untouched. The king then removed Daniel and placed his persecutors in his place. The hungry lions quickly devoured the persecutors.

The Birth of Jesus

The angel of the Lord appeared to Joseph and told him that Mary was with child by the power of God. This child was to be called Jesus. Mary and Joseph could not find shelter and stayed in a stable in Bethlehem where Jesus was born.

Jesus Preaches

Upon gathering his disciples and the crowds, Jesus taught them the Beatitudes, the Old Law and the New. the Golden Rule, the Power of Prayer, Purity of Intention, and avoiding Judgment.

Peter Walks on Water

When Peter saw Jesus walking on water towards his boat, he asked Jesus if he could come to Him. Jesus then commanded, "Come," and Peter did.

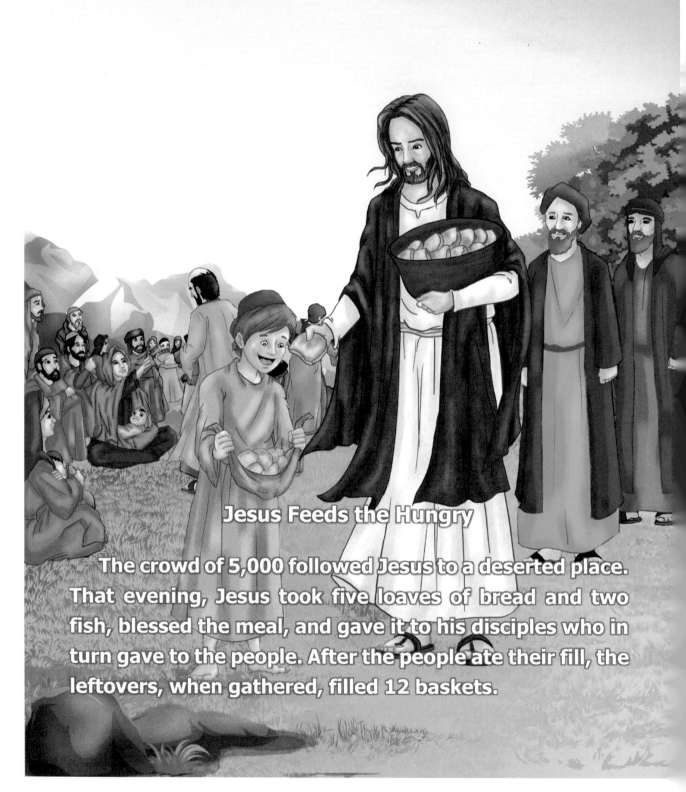

Jesus Feeds the Hungry

The crowd of 5,000 followed Jesus to a deserted place. That evening, Jesus took five loaves of bread and two fish, blessed the meal, and gave it to his disciples who in turn gave to the people. After the people ate their fill, the leftovers, when gathered, filled 12 baskets.

Jesus Blesses the Children

Children were brought to Jesus for Him to place his hands on them in prayer. The disciples began to scold the children. Jesus then said, "Let the children come to me. Do not hinder them. The kingdom of God belongs to them."

Jesus in the Temple

Every year, the Jews went to Jerusalem during the feast of Passover. At age 12, Jesus attended the feast with his family. After the feast was over Joseph and Mary noticed that Jesus had remained in Jerusalem. They returned to the city and found Jesus with the elder teachers, listening, and asking them questions.

Jesus Speaks to Everyone

Jesus toured all of Galilee, taught in their synagogues, proclaimed the good news of the kingdom, and cured the people of every disease and illness. His reputation was known beyond the area he traveled.

Jesus Meets Zacchaeus

Zacchaeus lived in Jericho and because he was a tax collector, he was considered a sinner. Jesus asked for permission to stay in his house and Zacchaeus accepted. Afterwards, Zacchaeus repented and vowed to give away half of his wealth and repay anyone he had cheated. This was Jesus' way of seeking out and saving the sinner.

The Good Shepherd

Jesus proclaims He is the ship gate. The one who enters through the gate is shepherd of the sheep. Whoever enters through Him will be safe.

The Last Supper

Jesus broke the bread and gave it to his disciples. Then, he poured them wine. He told them that the bread was a symbol of his body and the wine was a symbol of his blood which would be poured out for their sins to be forgiven.

Jesus Dies

From noon to midafternoon, there was darkness over the land. Toward midafternoon, Jesus cried in a loud voice, "My Lord, my God, why have you forsaken me?" Then once again, Jesus cried out, and gave up his spirit. Suddenly, the earth quaked, boulders split, and tombs opened.

The Resurrection

The body of Jesus lay two days in the tomb. On the morning of the third day, there was an earthquake and the appearance of an angel who rolled the stone from the mouth of the tomb. Jesus came forth from the tomb.

THE AUTHOR

A.M. Vela and his wife, **Mary Esparza-Vela**, are award-winning authors who have published various picture books and short stories. A number of their books received *Book of the Year Awards, National Finalist Awards, Family Choice Awards, Moonbeam Awards*, and *Five-Star Award Seals*. Their picture books are entertaining and deal with subjects like bullying, lost teeth, crossed eyes, acceptance, fears, patience, disabilities, overeating, responsibility, teasing, faith, imagination, respect, cleanliness, pets, etc.

Due to a demand for Spanish-language books, they have started writing and publishing bilingual and Spanish books. You are welcome to see them on their website www.readingforfun.net under the heading: **Spanish/ Bilingual Books**.

Made in the USA
Lexington, KY
31 October 2019